Math Workbook For кɪds With Dyscalculia

A resource toolkit book with 100 math activities to help overcome dyslexia with numbers

Volume 5

EasyMathGrowth

Introduction

Dyscalculia does not assume that the child does not have the ability to learn mathematics, but rather that the child has a different way of receiving, processing, interpreting mathematical information and therefore, it can and should be corrected with adequate stimulation. Through a specific re-education itinerary that encourages the formation of mental connections, dyscalculia can be overcome.

Dyscalculia must be treated in a very personalized way with each child, making a specific itinerary for each student based on the neuropsychological evaluation that allows knowing what the specific needs of the child are. The intervention by a professional focuses on a cognitive reeducation itinerary with the aim of stimulating or creating a new neural connection responsible for number concepts and number sense.

Ways to help your child with math:

1. Use the exercises to strengthen their number sense. These are basic number exercises such as simple operations, quantities and so on. You will find many of these in this book.

2. Use number games. Using games provides a fun sense that favors stimulation and learning.

3. Work with your child or student, basic mathematical concepts such as quantity, proportion (greater, less, much, little ...) and serialization.

4. Lean on visual references that help them understand mathematics (charts, drawings, diagrams ...)

5. Teach your child or student the correspondence between operations and mathematical language (add: union; subtract: remove; multiply: add the same number; divide: distribution)

6. Help them to visualize the problems and to unravel the facts and questions.

7. Train mental math through repeated activities so you will be giving the child with dyscalculia cognitive strategies for math.

8. It is very important that you always give the child the time they need to learn and create the relevant neural substrate.

9. Take care of the emotional well-being of the child. It is key that you offer emotional support to avoid derived problems.

10. Adapt the learning process to each child, at their level, their knowledge, their starting needs, etc.

Table of Contents

Table of Contents

NUMBERS

In this chapter, students will learn to:

- Count to and across 99 forward and backwards, begining with 0, 1 or any given number.

- Read, and write to 99 in numetrals and words.

- Place value, expanded form, identify smaller or larger number, sort odd and even numbers, and use <, >, = signs,

- Count numbers more than 100.

-Count to and across 999, forward and backwards, begining with 0, 1 or any given number.

- Place value, identify smaller or larger number, and use <, >, = signs.

- Skip Count by 2's, 3's, and 10's.

-Use ordinal numbers.

Missing Numbers

Help the kids reach their home by filling in the empty spaces.

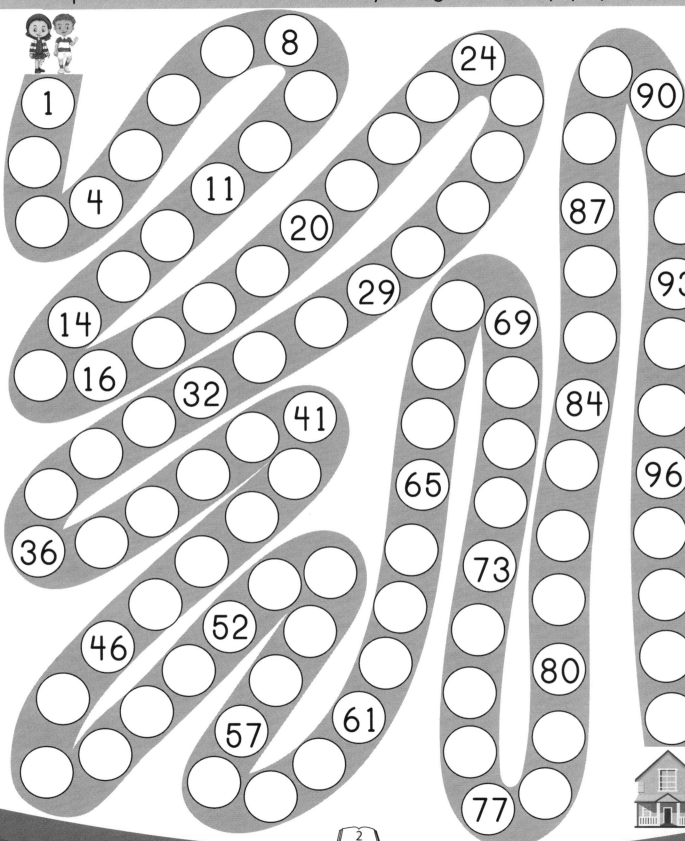

Place Value

(1) 10

_____ Tens, _____ Ones

(2) 40

_____ Tens, _____ Ones

(3) 54

_____ Tens, _____ Ones

(4) 76

_____ Tens, _____ Ones

(5) 37

_____ Tens, _____ Ones

(6) 78

_____ Tens, _____ Ones

Write the value that each underlined digit represents.

(1) 3̲6 ⟶ _____

(2) 4̲2 ⟶ _____

(3) 5̲0̲ ⟶ _____

(4) 6̲5 ⟶ _____

(5) 69̲ ⟶ _____

(6) 91̲ ⟶ _____

3

Expanded Form

Count the tens and ones and write the expanded form.

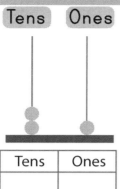

Tens	Ones

____ + ____ = _____

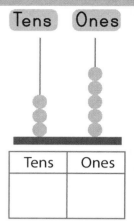

Tens	Ones

____ + ____ = _____

Tens	Ones

____ + ____ = _____

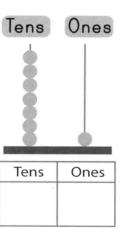

Tens	Ones

____ + ____ = _____

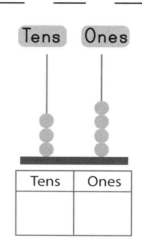

Tens	Ones

____ + ____ = _____

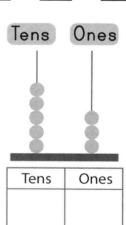

Tens	Ones

____ + ____ = _____

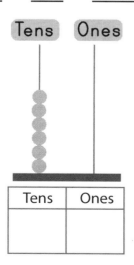

Tens	Ones

____ + ____ = _____

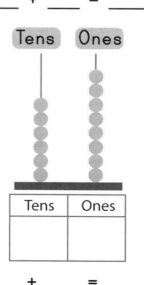

Tens	Ones

____ + ____ = _____

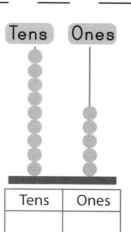

Tens	Ones

____ + ____ = _____

Ascending Order

Write the numbers in ascending order.

 1) 8, 3, 5   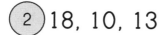 2) 18, 10, 13   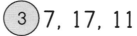 3) 7, 17, 11    4) 29, 23, 30

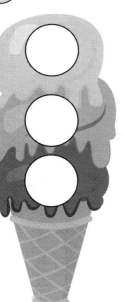   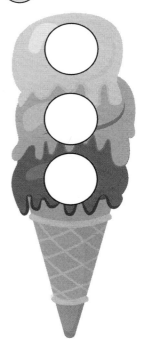

 5) 65, 55, 50    6) 73, 70, 67    7) 38, 85, 83   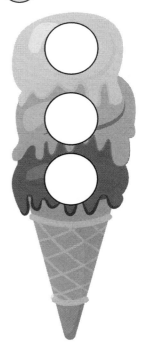 8) 78, 98, 89

Descending Order

① 6, 7, 2   ② 15, 14, 19   ③ 12, 20, 13   ④ 24, 30, 22

⑤ 45, 54, 52   ⑥ 79, 66, 56   ⑦ 72, 78, 88   ⑧ 49, 94, 79

Ascending/ Descending Order

Color the stairs with numbers in ascending order green.
Color the stairs with numbers in descending order pink.

1
| 4 |
| 7 |
| 8 |
| 10 |

2
| 11 |
| 13 |
| 15 |
| 18 |

3
| 22 |
| 20 |
| 17 |
| 13 |

4
| 13 |
| 23 |
| 33 |
| 43 |

5
| 39 |
| 35 |
| 31 |
| 30 |

6
| 42 |
| 47 |
| 51 |
| 55 |

7
| 66 |
| 62 |
| 26 |
| 22 |

8
| 32 |
| 35 |
| 53 |
| 59 |

9
| 57 |
| 65 |
| 75 |
| 79 |

10
| 54 |
| 45 |
| 44 |
| 40 |

11
| 48 |
| 58 |
| 68 |
| 78 |

12
| 99 |
| 92 |
| 89 |
| 86 |

Before, After, and Between

Write the number that comes before.

1. 33 34
2. 51 52
3. 70 71
4. 86 87

Write the number that comes after.

1. 45 46
2. 28 29
2. 64 65
4. 82 83

Write the number that comes in between.

1. 19 21
2. 50 52
3. 85 87
4. 93 95

Greater or Less

Read each number and write the sign <, >, or = in the circle.

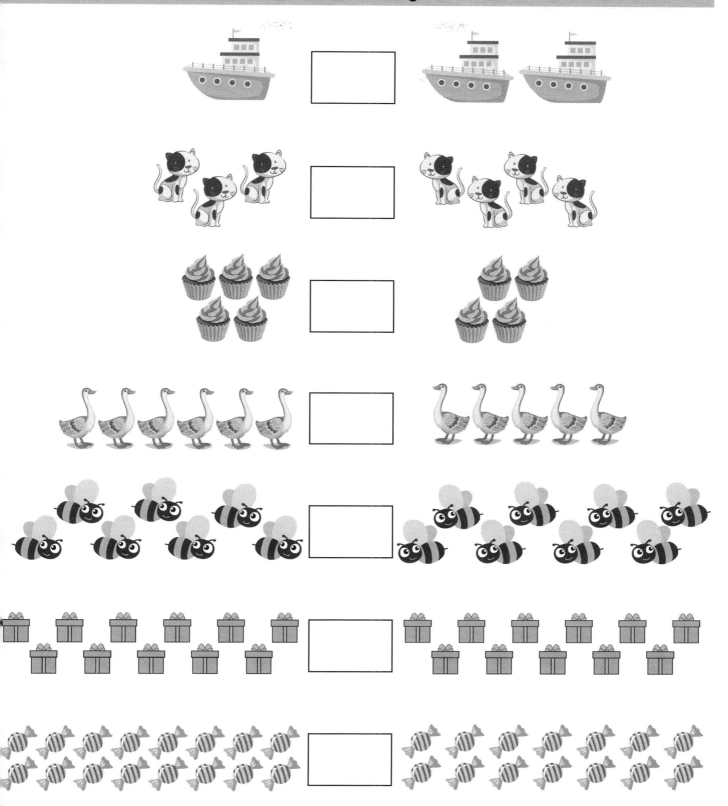

Odd Numbers

Help the cat collect the balls that only have odd numbers by drawing the path from start to end.

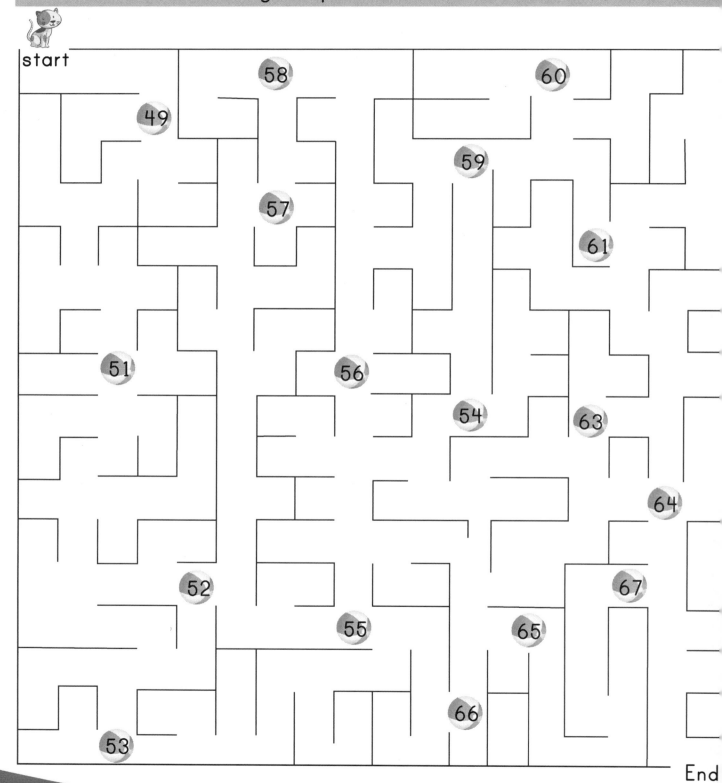

start

End

Even Numbers

Help the dog collect the balls that only have even numbers by drawing the path from start to end.

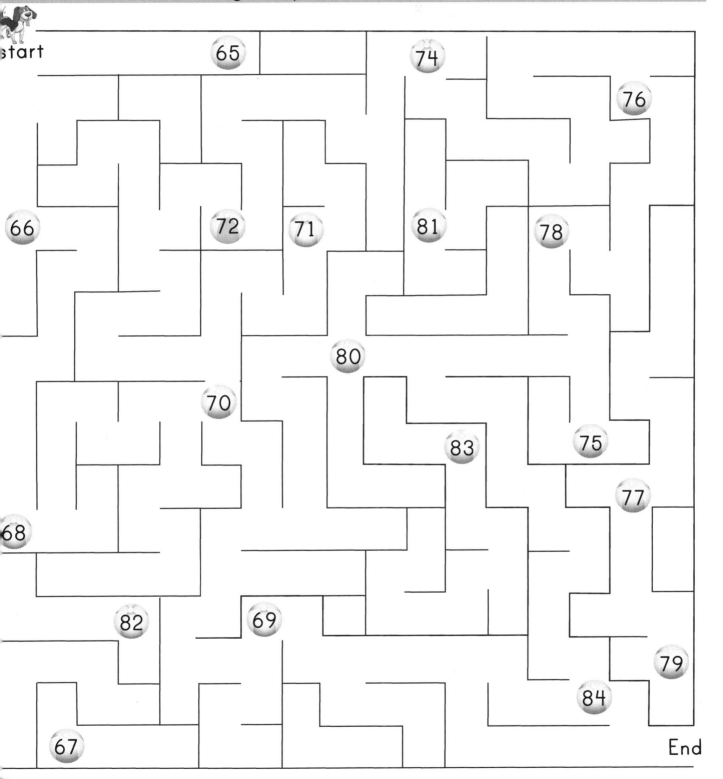

Odd and Even Numbers

Color the boxes with odd numbers purple.
Color the boxes with even numbers yellow.

1	2	3	4	5	6	7	8	9	10
11	12	13	14	15	16	17	18	19	20
21	22	23	24	25	26	27	28	29	30
31	32	33	34	35	36	37	38	39	40
41	42	43	44	45	46	47	48	49	50
51	52	53	54	55	56	57	58	59	60
61	62	63	64	65	66	67	68	69	70
71	72	73	74	75	76	77	78	79	80
81	82	83	84	85	86	87	88	89	90
91	92	93	94	95	96	97	98	99	100

Counting in Words

	Six	Seven
	Thirteen	Fourteen

	Twenty -Two	Twenty -Three
	Twenty -Nine	Thirty

	Thirty -Four	Twenty -Five
	Forty -One	Forty -Two

Write the number that comes after.

One	Two	
Nine	Ten	

Seventeen	Eighteen	
Twenty -Five	Twenty -Six	

Thirty -Eight	Thirty -Nine	
Forty -Eight	Forty -Nine	

Write the number that comes in between.

Three		Five
Eleven		Thirteen

Nineteen		Twenty -One
Twenty -Four		Twenty -Six

Thirty -Seven		Thirty -Nine
Forty -Two		Forty -Four

Numbers More Than 100

Read the number line and fill in the blanks.

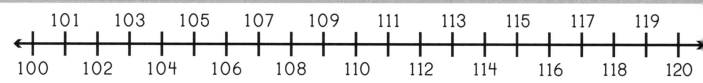

(1) 1 hundred and 1 = 101

(2) 1 hundred and 2 = [ ]

(3) 1 hundred and 3 = [ ]

(4) 1 hundred and 9 = [ ]

(5) 1 hundred and 11 = [ ]

(6) 1 hundred and 20 = [ ]

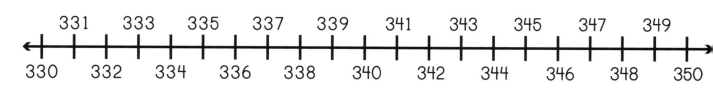

(7) 3 hundred and 30 = [ ]

(8) 3 hundred and 36 = [ ]

(9) 3 hundred and 40 = [ ]

(10) 3 hundred and 42 = [ ]

(11) 3 hundred and 47 = [ ]

(12) 3 hundred and 50 = [ ]

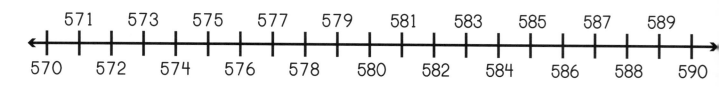

(13) 5 hundred and 73 = [ ]

(14) 5 hundred and 75 = [ ]

(15) 5 hundred and 80 = [ ]

(16) 5 hundred and 87 = [ ]

Place Value (More Than 100)

1 105

___ Hundred, ___ Tens, ___ Ones

2 132

___ Hundred, ___ Tens, ___ Ones

3 534

___ Hundred, ___ Tens, ___ Ones

4 248

___ Hundred, ___ Tens, ___ Ones

5 687

___ Hundred, ___ Tens, ___ Ones

6 650

___ Hundred, ___ Tens, ___ Ones

Write the value that each underlined digit represents.

1 3̲64 ⟶ _____

2 4̲25 ⟶ _____

3 50̲6 ⟶ _____

4 685̲ ⟶ _____

5 679̲ ⟶ _____

6 9̲01 ⟶ _____

Expanded Form (More than 100)

Count the hundreds, tens, and ones and write the expanded form.

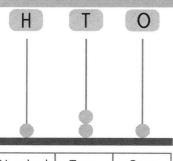

Hundreds	Tens	Ones

___ + ___ + ___ = ___

Hundreds	Tens	Ones

___ + ___ + ___ = ___

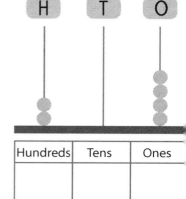

Hundreds	Tens	Ones

___ + ___ + ___ = ___

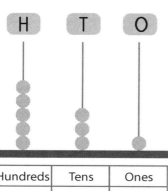

Hundreds	Tens	Ones

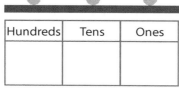

___ + ___ + ___ = ___

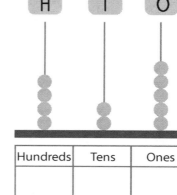

Hundreds	Tens	Ones

___ + ___ + ___ = ___

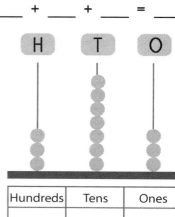

Hundreds	Tens	Ones

___ + ___ + ___ = ___

Hundreds	Tens	Ones

___ + ___ + ___ = ___

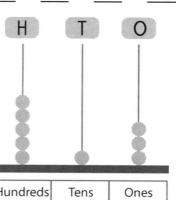

Hundreds	Tens	Ones

___ + ___ + ___ = ___

Hundreds	Tens	Ones

___ + ___ + ___ = ___

Ascending Order

1) 108, 103, 104

2) 147, 150, 163

3) 219, 214, 241

4) 465, 355, 350

5) 673, 770, 767

6) 838, 995, 983

 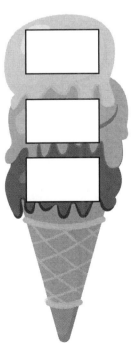 

Descending Order

(1) 140, 104, 114   (2) 115, 134, 129   (3) 312, 220, 321

(4) 445, 254, 532   (5) 479, 606, 556   (6) 772, 768, 878

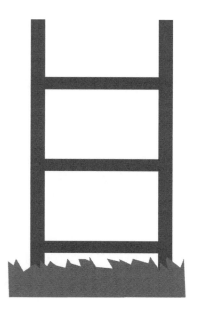  

Ascending/ Descending Order

Color the stairs with numbers in ascending order orange.
Color the stairs with numbers in descending order blue.

1
103
109
118
120

2
111
123
215
328

3
322
220
117
103

4
113
223
333
443

5
539
535
431
430

6
442
547
551
655

7
646
632
236
212

8
132
235
353
359

9
357
565
775
879

10
654
645
444
240

11
548
658
768
978

12
999
892
889
786

Before, After, and Between

Write the number that comes before.

1. ___ 104 105
2. ___ 251 252
3. ___ 730 731
4. ___ 846 847

Write the number that comes after.

1. 459 460 ___
2. 208 209 ___

2. 641 642 ___
4. 852 853 ___

Write the number that comes in between.

1. 119 ___ 121
2. 550 ___ 552

3. 815 ___ 817
4. 933 ___ 935

Compare Numbers

Write greater than, less than or equal to.
Then write the sign <, > or =.

(1) 25 is _____ 43

$\underline{}\; 25 \;\underline{}$ ☐ $\underline{}\; 43 \;\underline{}$

(2) 33 is _____ 19

$\underline{}\; 33 \;\underline{}$ ☐ $\underline{}\; 19 \;\underline{}$

(3) 53 is _____ 35

$\underline{}\; 53 \;\underline{}$ ☐ $\underline{}\; 35 \;\underline{}$

(4) 45 is _____ 78

$\underline{}\; 45 \;\underline{}$ ☐ $\underline{}\; 78 \;\underline{}$

(5) 89 is _____ 78

$\underline{}\; 8z9 \;\underline{}$ ☐ $\underline{}\; 78 \;\underline{}$

(6) 60 is _____ 61

$\underline{}\; 60 \;\underline{}$ ☐ $\underline{}\; 61 \;\underline{}$

(7) 252 is _____ 443

$\underline{}\; 252 \;\underline{}$ ☐ $\underline{}\; 443 \;\underline{}$

(8) 354 is _____ 143

$\underline{}\; 354 \;\underline{}$ ☐ $\underline{}\; 143 \;\underline{}$

(9) 964 is _____ 469

$\underline{}\; 964 \;\underline{}$ ☐ $\underline{}\; 469 \;\underline{}$

(10) 890 is _____ 713

$\underline{}\; 890 \;\underline{}$ ☐ $\underline{}\; 713 \;\underline{}$

Skip Counting by 2's

Skip Counting by 3's

Connect the dots by skip counting by 3's

Skip Counting by 2's and 3's

Help the dog hop by two to reach his home.

Start

19	20	21	22	23	24	25	26	27	28	29

| | | | | | | | | | | 30 |

42	41	40	39	38	37	36	35	34	33	32	31

| 43 | | | | | | | | | | | |

End

44	45	46	47	48	49	50	51	52	53

Help the frog leap by three to land on the lily pad.

Start

11	12	13	14	15	16	17	18	19	20	21

| | | | | | | | | | | 22 |

34	33	32	31	30	29	28	27	26	25	24	23

| 35 | | | | | | | | | | | |

End

36	37	38	39	40	41	42	43	44	45

Skip Counting by 10's

Fill in the caterpillar by skip counting by tens.

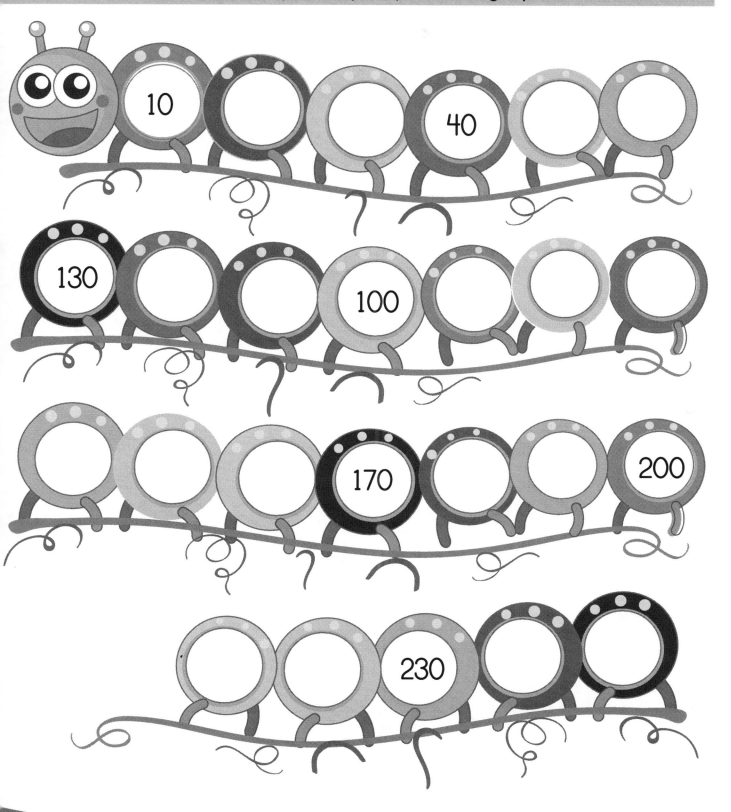

Ordinal Numbers

Fill in the blanks by writing the ordinal number of each animal.

Start here!

_____

_____

_____

_____

_____

_____

_____

Ordinal Numbers

First, Fourth, Tenth = Red

Second, Fifth, Nineth = Blue

Third, Sixth, Eighth = Yellow

Seventh, 11th, Fifteenth = Green

Fourteenth, Nineteenth, 12th = Pink

Thirteenth, Seventeenth = Orange

16th, Eighteenth, Twentieth = Purple

NUMBER OPERATIONS

In this chapter, students will learn to:

- Make number bonds.

-Make doubles and doubles plus one, solve commutative addition.

-Solve one-digit and two-digit addition, with or without carry, addition word problems, mental math, and estimate sums.

- Solve one-digit and two-digit subtraction, with or without borrowing, subtraction word problems, and estimate differences.

- Solve repeated addition and multiplication, simple multiplication, and commutative multiplication using concrete objects and pictorial representations.

-Solve repeated subtraction and division, simple division problems using concrete objects and pictorial representations.

Count on 1, 2, and 3

(1) 1 + 1 = _____

(2) 2 + 1 = _____

(3) 3 + 1 = _____

(4) 4 + 1 = _____

(5) 5 + 1 = _____

(6) 6 + 1 = _____

(7) 7 + 1 = _____

(8) 8 + 1 = _____

(9) 9 + 1 = _____

(10) 1 + 2 = _____

(11) 2 + 2 = _____

(12) 3 + 2 = _____

(13) 4 + 2 = _____

(14) 5 + 2 = _____

(15) 6 + 2 = _____

(16) 7 + 2 = _____

(17) 8 + 2 = _____

(18) 9 + 2 = _____

(19) 1 + 3 = _____

(20) 2 + 3 = _____

(21) 3 + 3 = _____

(22) 4 + 3 = _____

(23) 5 + 3 = _____

(24) 6 + 3 = _____

(25) 7 + 3 = _____

(26) 8 + 3 = _____

(27) 9 + 3 = _____

Number Bonds of 4, 5, and 6

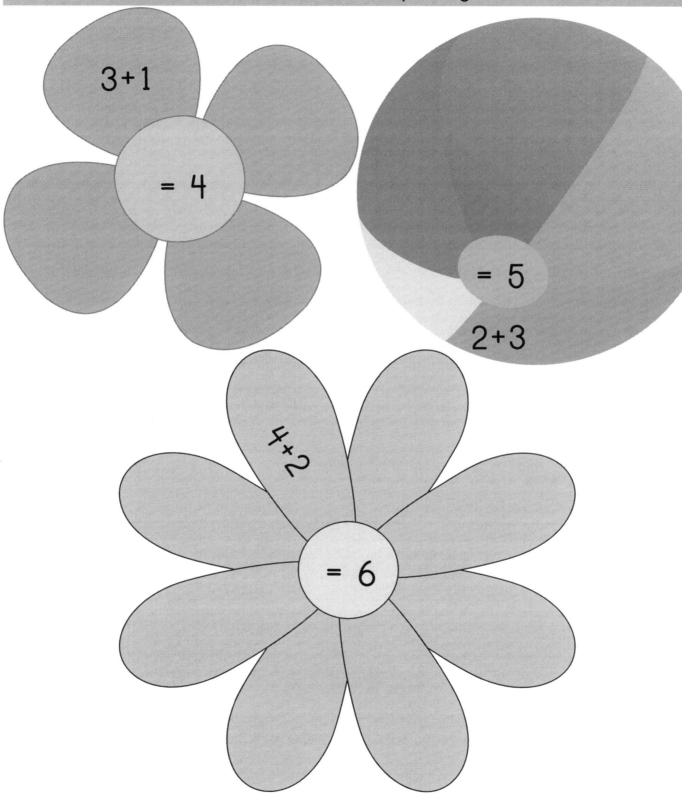

3+1

= 4

= 5

2+3

4+2

= 6

Doubles and Doubles Plus One

Complete the addition table.

Write the doubles sum blue.

Write the doubles plus one orange.

+	0	1	2	3	4	5	6	7	8	9
0										
1										
2										
3										
4										
5										
6										
7										
8										
9										

Number Bonds of 7, 8, and 9

Write all of the different ways to get 7, 8, and 9.

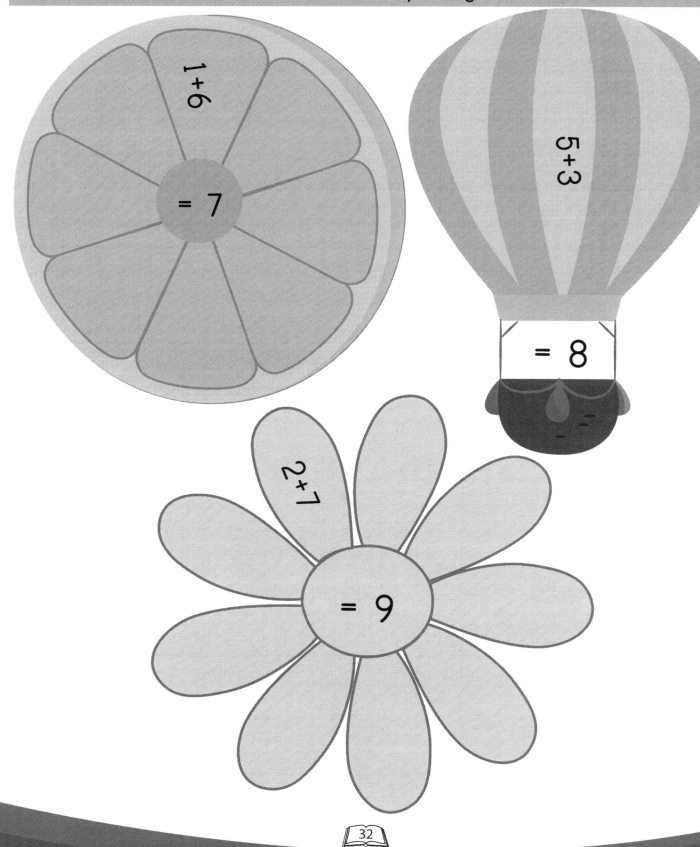

1+6

= 7

5+3

= 8

2+7

= 9

Commutative Addition

1
$1 + 2 =$ ⟨ 3
$2 + 1 =$ ⟨ 3 ⟩

2
$2 + 3 =$ _____
$3 + 2 =$ _____

3
$3 + 6 =$ _____
$6 + 3 =$ _____

4
$4 + 1 =$ _____
$1 + 4 =$ _____

5
$5 + 3 =$ _____
$3 + 5 =$ _____

6
$5 + 6 =$ _____
$6 + 5 =$ _____

7
$6 + 4 =$ _____
$4 + 6 =$ _____

8
$4 + 3 =$ _____
$3 + 4 =$ _____

9
$5 + 2 =$ _____
$2 + 5 =$ _____

10
$7 + 2 =$ _____
$2 + 7 =$ _____

11
$6 + 7 =$ _____
$7 + 6 =$ _____

12
$5 + 4 =$ _____
$4 + 5 =$ _____

13
$6 + 8 =$ _____
$8 + 6 =$ _____

14
$7 + 3 =$ _____
$3 + 7 =$ _____

Number Bonds of 10

Write all of the different ways to get 10.

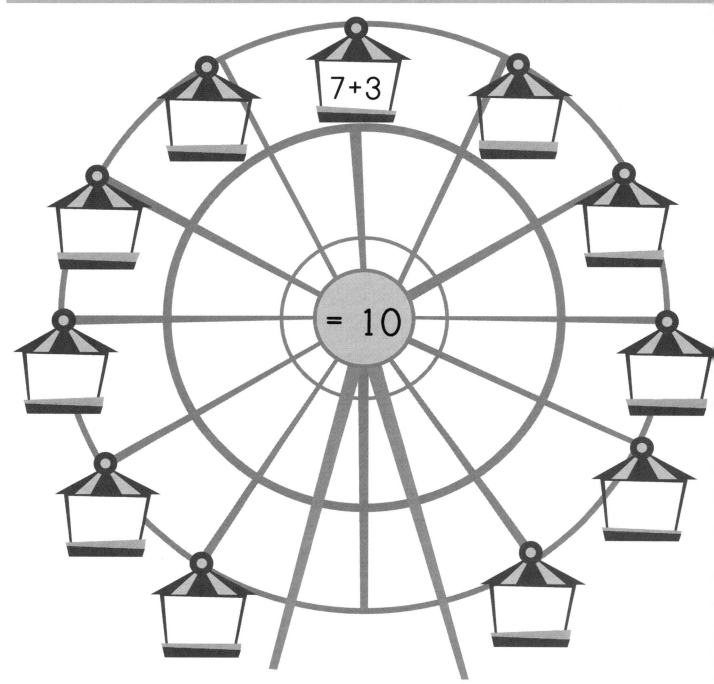

Color by Addition

Add and color the areas on the pineapple which sum matches the number on the leaves.

One-digit Addition

(1)
$$\begin{array}{r} 5 \\ + \quad 3 \\ \hline \end{array}$$

(2)
$$\begin{array}{r} 2 \\ + \quad 7 \\ \hline \end{array}$$

(3)
$$\begin{array}{r} 1 \\ + \quad 3 \\ \hline \end{array}$$

(4)
$$\begin{array}{r} 8 \\ + \quad 1 \\ \hline \end{array}$$

(5)
$$\begin{array}{r} 4 \\ + \quad 2 \\ \hline \end{array}$$

(6)
$$\begin{array}{r} 4 \\ + \quad 4 \\ \hline \end{array}$$

(7)
$$\begin{array}{r} 6 \\ + \quad 3 \\ \hline \end{array}$$

(8)
$$\begin{array}{r} 7 \\ + \quad 2 \\ \hline \end{array}$$

(9)
$$\begin{array}{r} 3 \\ + \quad 4 \\ \hline \end{array}$$

(10)
$$\begin{array}{r} 3 \\ + \quad 6 \\ \hline \end{array}$$

(11)
$$\begin{array}{r} 5 \\ + \quad 4 \\ \hline \end{array}$$

(12)
$$\begin{array}{r} 6 \\ + \quad 2 \\ \hline \end{array}$$

(13)
$$\begin{array}{r} 8 \\ + \quad 2 \\ \hline \end{array}$$

(14)
$$\begin{array}{r} 6 \\ + \quad 4 \\ \hline \end{array}$$

(15)
$$\begin{array}{r} 3 \\ + \quad 8 \\ \hline \end{array}$$

Addition-Word Problems

Solve the following problems and complete the number bonds.

1. Austin bought 2 red apples and 4 green apples. How many apples did he buy?

    ___ (+) ___ = ___

    _6_ apples

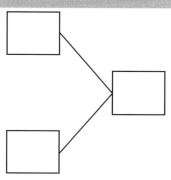

2. There are 5 bears in the zoo. 3 more join in. How many bears are there in all?

    ___ ◯ ___ = ___

    ___ bears

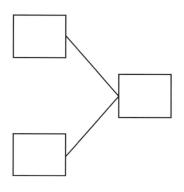

3. Mary has 6 balls. She got 4 more. How many balls does she have altogether?

    ___ ◯ ___ = ___

    ___ balls

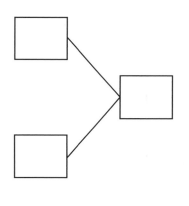

4. Minal planted 9 lemon seeds and 3 carrot seeds. How many seeds did she plant altogether?

    ___ ◯ ___ = ___

    ___ seeds

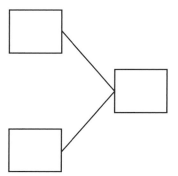

Add Tens

1
```
     1          1 tens          10
   + 2        + 2 tens        + 20
  _____      _____        _____
               _____ tens
```

2
```
     2          2 tens          20
   + 3        + 3 tens        + 30
  _____      _____        _____
               _____ tens
```

3
```
     5          5 tens          50
   + 1        + 1 tens        + 10
  _____      _____        _____
               _____ tens
```

4
```
     3          3 tens          30
   + 5        + 5 tens        + 50
  _____      _____        _____
               _____ tens
```

5
```
     6          6 tens          60
   + 2        + 2 tens        + 20
  _____      _____        _____
               _____ tens
```

6
```
     2          2 tens          20
   + 2        + 2 tens        + 20
  _____      _____        _____
               _____ tens
```

7
```
     4          4 tens          40
   + 3        + 3 tens        + 30
  _____      _____        _____
               _____ tens
```

8
```
     3          3 tens          30
   + 3        + 3 tens        + 30
  _____      _____        _____
               _____ tens
```

9
```
     5          5 tens          50
   + 4        + 4 tens        + 40
  _____      _____        _____
               _____ tens
```

10
```
     3          3 tens          30
   + 6        + 6 tens        + 60
  _____      _____        _____
               _____ tens
```

Two-digit Addition

Numbers	Add the ones. Are there 10 or more ones? If so, regroup 10 ones as 1 tens		Write how many tens and ones.
14 + 16	Yes	No	_____ tens _____ ones
18 + 23	Yes	No	_____ tens _____ ones
21 + 19	Yes	No	_____ tens _____ ones
35 + 26	Yes	No	_____ tens _____ ones
44 + 22	Yes	No	_____ tens _____ ones
47 + 37	Yes	No	_____ tens _____ ones
55 + 64	Yes	No	_____ tens _____ ones
43 + 45	Yes	No	_____ tens _____ ones

Two-digit Addition

Add the following numbers.

1 | Tens | Ones
□
```
   1   6
+  1   5
───────────
```

2 | Tens | Ones
□
```
   1   4
+  1   7
───────────
```

3 | Tens | One
□
```
   2   7
+  1   3
───────────
```

4 | Tens | Ones
□
```
   1   8
+  1   3
───────────
```

5 | Tens | Ones
□
```
   1   9
+  2   1
───────────
```

6 | Tens | One
□
```
   1   6
+  1   4
───────────
```

7 | Tens | Ones
□
```
   1   7
+  2   3
───────────
```

8 | Tens | Ones
□
```
   1   7
+  2   4
───────────
```

9 | Tens | One
□
```
   1   5
+  2   5
───────────
```

10 | Tens | Ones
□
```
   1   6
+  1   7
───────────
```

11 | Tens | Ones
□
```
   2   7
+  1   5
───────────
```

12 | Tens | Ones
□
```
   1   6
+  2   5
───────────
```

Addition Word Problems

Read the following statements and add the numbers.

1. One box holds 28 baseballs. Another box holds 33 baseballs. How many baseballs are there altogether?

   ___ baseballs

Tens	Ones
□	
2	8
+ 3	3

2. There are 35 beans in the bottle. Bella added 21 more. How many beans are there altogether?

   ___ beans

Tens	Ones
□	
3	5
+ 2	1

3. There are 25 men and 37 women on a bus. How many people are there in all?

   ___ people

Tens	Ones
□	
2	5
+ 3	7

4. There are 43 oranges and 38 strawberries. How many fruits are there in all?

   ___ fruits

Tens	Ones
□	
4	3
+ 3	8

5. There are 56 peacocks and 46 pelican in a bird park. How many birds are there in all?

   ___ birds

Tens	Ones
□	
5	6
+ 4	6

Rewrite Two-digit Addtion

1 23 + 8

Tens Ones

☐

+ _____

_____

2 13 + 29

Tens Ones

☐

+ _____

_____

3 15 + 29

Tens Ones

☐

+ _____

_____

4 53 + 7

Tens Ones

☐

+ _____

_____

5 44 + 21

Tens Ones

☐

+ _____

_____

6 37 + 19

Tens Ones

☐

+ _____

_____

7 59 + 18

Tens Ones

☐

+ _____

_____

8 57 + 34

Tens Ones

☐

+ _____

_____

9 35 + 54

Tens Ones

☐

+ _____

_____

10 67 + 9

Tens Ones

☐

+ _____

_____

11 73 + 68

Tens Ones

☐

+ _____

_____

12 65 + 55

Tens Ones

☐

+ _____

_____

Problem Solving - Estimate Sums

Use the number line to round. Add rounded numbers to get the estimated sum.

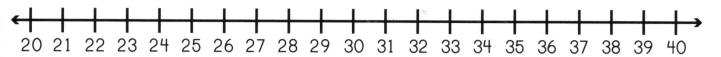

20 21 22 23 24 25 26 27 28 29 30 31 32 33 34 35 36 37 38 39 40

① There are 27 candies and 22 chocolates in the basket. How many snacks are there in total?

Tens	Ones
3	0
+ 2	0

____ snacks

② Emma has 33 pencils. Brenda gives her 29 pencils. How many pencils does she have in total?

Tens	Ones
+	

____ pencils

③ A bakery sold 21 cakes on Monday and 29 cakes on Tuesday. How many cakes did they sell in total?

Tens	Ones
+	

____ cakes

④ Sally has 32 books. He bought 29 more. How many books does he have in total?

Tens	Ones
+	

____ books

⑤ The fisherman caught 36 fish on Saturday. He caught 33 more on Sunday. How many fish did he catch in total?

Tens	Ones
+	

____ fish

Mental Math–Addition

① 23 + 52

Think!

Add the tens.
20 + 50 = 70
Then add the ones.
3 + 2 = 5
add the tens and ones.
70 + 5 = 75

② 22 + 35

___ + ___ = ___

___ + ___ = ___

___ + ___ = ___

③ 51 + 29

___ + ___ = ___

___ + ___ = ___

___ + ___ = ___

④ 43 + 72

___ + ___ = ___

___ + ___ = ___

___ + ___ = ___

⑤ 48 + 31

___ + ___ = ___

___ + ___ = ___

___ + ___ = ___

⑥ 51 + 22

___ + ___ = ___

___ + ___ = ___

___ + ___ = ___

⑦ 34 + 26

___ + ___ = ___

___ + ___ = ___

___ + ___ = ___

⑧ 32 + 48

___ + ___ = ___

___ + ___ = ___

___ + ___ = ___

⑨ 35 + 45

___ + ___ = ___

___ + ___ = ___

___ + ___ = ___

⑩ 67 + 23

___ + ___ = ___

___ + ___ = ___

___ + ___ = ___

⑪ 43 + 33

___ + ___ = ___

___ + ___ = ___

___ + ___ = ___

⑫ 21 + 75

___ + ___ = ___

___ + ___ = ___

___ + ___ = ___

Subtract All or None

Subtract the following numbers.

1) How many birds are left?

```
    5
-   5
_____
```

2) How many birds are left?

```
    5
-   0
_____
```

3)
```
    3
-   3
_____
```

4)
```
   15
-   0
_____
```

5)
```
    8
-   8
_____
```

6)
```
    5
-   0
_____
```

7)
```
   24
-  24
_____
```

8)
```
   17
-   0
_____
```

9)
```
   39
-  39
_____
```

10)
```
   51
-   0
_____
```

11)
```
   29
-  29
_____
```

12)
```
   34
-   0
_____
```

13)
```
   48
-   0
_____
```

14)
```
   55
-  55
_____
```

Count Back

(1) 4 - 2 = _____   (2) 6 - 1 = _____

(3) 8 - 3 = _____   (4) 5 - 2 = _____

(5)
```
    8
-   1
____
```

(6)
```
    4
-   3
____
```

(7)
```
    4
-   4
____
```

(8)
```
    6
-   3
____
```

(9)
```
    9
-   2
____
```

(10)
```
    7
-   4
____
```

(11)
```
    8
-   6
____
```

(12)
```
    5
-   4
____
```

(13)
```
    6
-   2
____
```

(14)
```
    9
-   5
____
```

(15)
```
    8
-   4
____
```

(16)
```
    8
-   5
____
```

Subtract Tens

(1)

$$\begin{array}{r} 2 \\ -\ 1 \\ \hline \end{array}$$

$$\begin{array}{r} 2\ tens \\ -\ 1\ tens \\ \hline tens \end{array}$$

$$\begin{array}{r} 20 \\ -\ 10 \\ \hline \end{array}$$

(2)

$$\begin{array}{r} 3 \\ -\ 2 \\ \hline \end{array}$$

$$\begin{array}{r} 3\ tens \\ -\ 2\ tens \\ \hline tens \end{array}$$

$$\begin{array}{r} 30 \\ -\ 20 \\ \hline \end{array}$$

(3)

$$\begin{array}{r} 4 \\ -\ 1 \\ \hline \end{array}$$

$$\begin{array}{r} 4\ tens \\ -\ 1\ tens \\ \hline tens \end{array}$$

$$\begin{array}{r} 40 \\ -\ 10 \\ \hline \end{array}$$

(4)

$$\begin{array}{r} 5 \\ -\ 3 \\ \hline \end{array}$$

$$\begin{array}{r} 5\ tens \\ -\ 3\ tens \\ \hline tens \end{array}$$

$$\begin{array}{r} 50 \\ -\ 30 \\ \hline \end{array}$$

(5)

$$\begin{array}{r} 6 \\ -\ 2 \\ \hline \end{array}$$

$$\begin{array}{r} 6\ tens \\ -\ 2\ tens \\ \hline tens \end{array}$$

$$\begin{array}{r} 60 \\ -\ 20 \\ \hline \end{array}$$

(6)

$$\begin{array}{r} 2 \\ -\ 2 \\ \hline \end{array}$$

$$\begin{array}{r} 2\ tens \\ -\ 2\ tens \\ \hline tens \end{array}$$

$$\begin{array}{r} 20 \\ -\ 20 \\ \hline \end{array}$$

(7)

$$\begin{array}{r} 4 \\ -\ 3 \\ \hline \end{array}$$

$$\begin{array}{r} 4\ tens \\ -\ 3\ tens \\ \hline tens \end{array}$$

$$\begin{array}{r} 40 \\ -\ 30 \\ \hline \end{array}$$

(8)

$$\begin{array}{r} 6 \\ -\ 3 \\ \hline \end{array}$$

$$\begin{array}{r} 6\ tens \\ -\ 3\ tens \\ \hline tens \end{array}$$

$$\begin{array}{r} 60 \\ -\ 30 \\ \hline \end{array}$$

(9)

$$\begin{array}{r} 7 \\ -\ 4 \\ \hline \end{array}$$

$$\begin{array}{r} 7\ tens \\ -\ 4\ tens \\ \hline tens \end{array}$$

$$\begin{array}{r} 70 \\ -\ 40 \\ \hline \end{array}$$

(10)

$$\begin{array}{r} 9 \\ -\ 6 \\ \hline \end{array}$$

$$\begin{array}{r} 9\ tens \\ -\ 6\ tens \\ \hline tens \end{array}$$

$$\begin{array}{r} 90 \\ -\ 60 \\ \hline \end{array}$$

Think Addition to Subtract

1
$\begin{array}{r} 5 \\ +\ 3 \\ \hline \end{array}$ $\begin{array}{r} \square\square \\ 11 \\ -\ 3 \\ \hline \end{array}$

2
$\begin{array}{r} 4 \\ +\ 6 \\ \hline \end{array}$ $\begin{array}{r} \square\square \\ 10 \\ -\ 6 \\ \hline \end{array}$

3
$\begin{array}{r} 2 \\ +\ 7 \\ \hline \end{array}$ $\begin{array}{r} 9 \\ -\ 7 \\ \hline \end{array}$

4
$\begin{array}{r} 14 \\ +\ 3 \\ \hline \end{array}$ $\begin{array}{r} \square\square \\ 17 \\ -\ 3 \\ \hline \end{array}$

5
$\begin{array}{r} 9 \\ +\ 8 \\ \hline \end{array}$ $\begin{array}{r} \square\square \\ 17 \\ -\ 8 \\ \hline \end{array}$

6
$\begin{array}{r} 15 \\ +\ 7 \\ \hline \end{array}$ $\begin{array}{r} \square\square \\ 22 \\ -\ 7 \\ \hline \end{array}$

7
$\begin{array}{r} 12 \\ +\ 6 \\ \hline \end{array}$ $\begin{array}{r} 18 \\ -\ 6 \\ \hline \end{array}$

8
$\begin{array}{r} 16 \\ +\ 8 \\ \hline \end{array}$ $\begin{array}{r} \square\square \\ 24 \\ -\ 8 \\ \hline \end{array}$

9
$\begin{array}{r} 26 \\ +\ 13 \\ \hline \end{array}$ $\begin{array}{r} 39 \\ -\ 13 \\ \hline \end{array}$

10 $3 + 1 =$ _____
$4 - 1 =$ _____

11 $4 + 8 =$ _____
$12 - 8 =$ _____

12 $7 + 7 =$ _____
$14 - 7 =$ _____

13 $10 + 4 =$ _____
$14 - 4 =$ _____

14 $13 + 6 =$ _____
$19 - 6 =$ _____

15 $12 + 9 =$ _____
$21 - 9 =$ _____

Think Addition to Subtract

Look at the signs (+ and -) and solve the following operations.

1) 8, 5, 3

5 + 3	8 - 3	5 + 3	8 - 5

2) 9, 7, 2

7 + 2	9 - 2	7 + 2	9 - 7

3) 11, 7, 4

7 + 4	11 - 4	7 + 4	11 - 7

4) 13, 5, 8

5 + 8	13 - 8	5 + 8	13 - 5

5) 14, 6, 8

6 + 8	14 - 8	6 + 8	14 - 6

6) 15, 9, 6

9 + 6	15 - 6	9 + 6	15 - 9

7) 18, 12, 6

12 + 6	18 - 6	12 + 6	18 - 12

8) 21, 13, 8

13 + 8	21 - 8	13 + 8	21 - 13

Two-digit Subtraction

Subtract the following numbers.

Numbers	Do you need to regroup?	Write how many tens and ones.
16 - 9	Yes　　　No	_____ tens _____ ones
23 - 18	Yes　　　No	_____ tens _____ ones
21 + 19	Yes　　　No	_____ tens _____ ones
35 - 26	Yes　　　No	_____ tens _____ ones
44 - 22	Yes　　　No	_____ tens _____ ones
48 - 37	Yes　　　No	_____ tens _____ ones
95 - 58	Yes　　　No	_____ tens _____ ones
83 - 45	Yes　　　No	_____ tens _____ ones

Two-digit Subtraction

Find two ways to make each number sentence true.

1   Tens   Ones

[5]   [10]

~~6~~   ~~0~~

−   1   5

_____

2   Tens   Ones

□   □

4   8

−   2   5

_____

3   Tens   Ones

□   □

4   4

−   2   8

_____

4   Tens   Ones

□   □

5   8

−   3   6

_____

5   Tens   Ones

□   □

5   5

−   4   9

_____

6   Tens   Ones

□   □

3   7

−   2   2

_____

7   Tens   Ones

□   □

6   7

−   4   8

_____

8   Tens   Ones

□   □

7   7

−   5   3

_____

9   Tens   Ones

□   □

8   5

−   3   2

_____

10   Tens   Ones

□   □

8   4

−   4   7

_____

11   Tens   Ones

□   □

9   1

−   1   5

_____

12   Tens   Ones

□   □

9   6

−   2   9

_____

Subtraction-Word Problems

1. Newton has 33 pens and Frazer has 28 pens. How many more pens does Newton have?

	Tens	Ones
	☐	☐
	3	3
−	2	8

___ pens

2. A music shop has 35 violins. 21 of them are sold. How many violins are there left?

	Tens	Ones
	3	5
−	2	1

___ violins

3. There are 56 balloons at a birthday party. 41 blew away. How many balloons are there left?

	Tens	Ones
	5	6
−	4	1

___ balloons

4. There are 76 pears in a shop. 50 of them are sold. How many pears are lthere eft?

	Tens	Ones
	7	6
−	5	0

___ pears

5. There were 95 frogs. 46 leap away. How many frogs are there left?

	Tens	Ones
	☐	☐
	9	5
−	4	6

___ frogs

Rewrite Two-digit Subtraction

Rewrite and subtract the numbers.

1 33 - 18

Tens Ones
□   □

-
_____

_____

2 56 - 28

Tens Ones
□   □

-
_____

_____

3 50 - 19

Tens Ones
□   □

-
_____

_____

4 67 - 29

Tens Ones
□   □

-
_____

_____

5 45 - 28

Tens Ones
□   □

-
_____

_____

6 51 - 32

Tens Ones
□   □

-
_____

_____

7 54 - 45

Tens Ones
□   □

-
_____

_____

8 75 - 29

Tens Ones
□   □

-
_____

_____

9 82 - 65

Tens Ones
□   □

-
_____

_____

10 67 - 39

Tens Ones
□   □

-
_____

_____

11 73 - 58

Tens Ones
□   □

-
_____

_____

12 94 - 56

Tens Ones
□   □

-
_____

_____

Problem Solving-Estimate Difference

Solve the following operations.

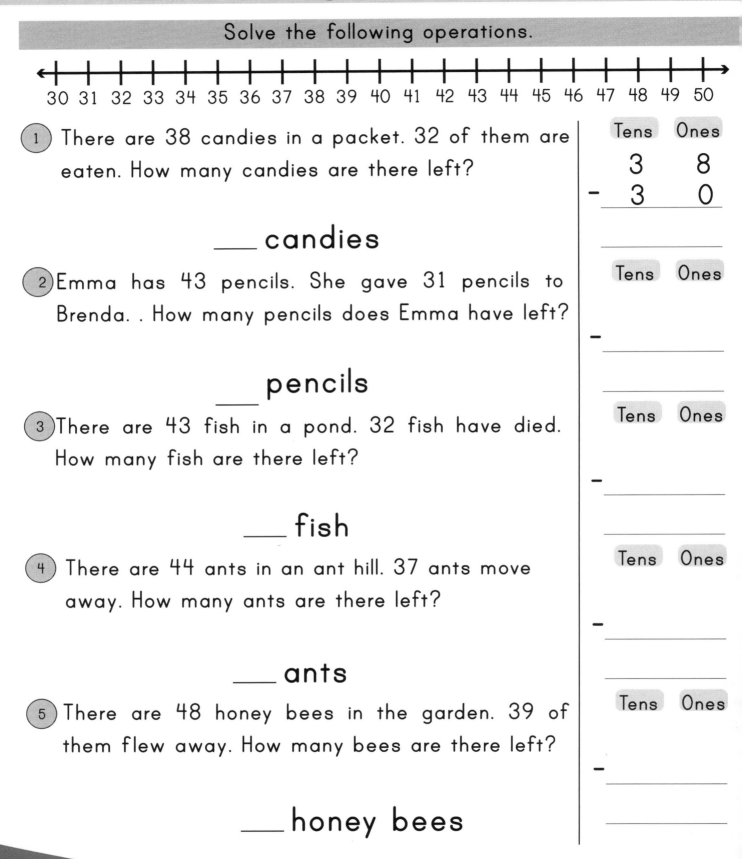

← | | | | | | | | | | | | | | | | | | | | | →
30 31 32 33 34 35 36 37 38 39 40 41 42 43 44 45 46 47 48 49 50

(1) There are 38 candies in a packet. 32 of them are eaten. How many candies are there left?

Tens	Ones
3	8
− 3	0

___ candies

(2) Emma has 43 pencils. She gave 31 pencils to Brenda. . How many pencils does Emma have left?

Tens	Ones
−	

___ pencils

(3) There are 43 fish in a pond. 32 fish have died. How many fish are there left?

Tens	Ones
−	

___ fish

(4) There are 44 ants in an ant hill. 37 ants move away. How many ants are there left?

Tens	Ones
−	

___ ants

(5) There are 48 honey bees in the garden. 39 of them flew away. How many bees are there left?

Tens	Ones
−	

___ honey bees

Explore Multiplication

Make equal groups by drawing equal number of shapes in each group.

1 Make 2 equal groups by drawing 3 ■ in each group.

Group 1	Group 2

_____ + _____ = _____

2 Make 3 equal groups by drawing 4 ▭ in each group.

Group 1	Group 2	Group 3

_____ + _____ + _____ = _____

3 Make 2 equal groups by drawing 5 ▲ in each group.

Group 1	Group 2

_____ + _____ = _____

4 Make 3 equal groups by drawing 6 ★ in each group.

Group 1	Group 2	Group 3

_____ + _____ + _____ = _____

Repeated Addition and Multiplication

Solve the following operations.

1 + 1 + 1 + 1 = _____   4 x 1 = _____

3 + 3 + 3 = _____   3 x 3 = _____

4 + 4 + 4 = _____   3 x 4 = _____

5 + 5 + 5 + 5 = _____   4 x 5 = _____

10 + 10 = _____   2 x 10 = _____

Multiplication Arrays

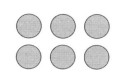

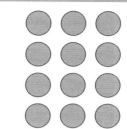

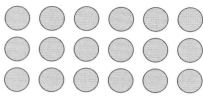

_____ rows

_____ in each row

2 x 3 = _____

_____ rows

_____ in each row

4 x 3 = _____

_____ rows

_____ in each row

3 x 6 = _____

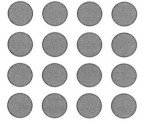

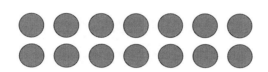

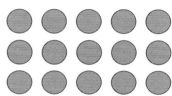

_____ rows

_____ in each row

4 x 4 = _____

_____ rows

_____ in each row

2 x 7 = _____

_____ rows

_____ in each row

3 x 5 = _____

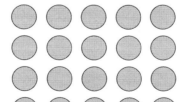

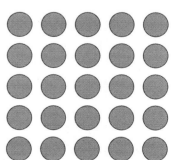

_____ rows

_____ in each row

2 x 4 = _____

_____ rows

_____ in each row

4 x 5 = _____

_____ rows

_____ in each row

5 x 5 = _____

Commutative Multiplication

1

$3 \times 2 = $ _____

_____ $\times$ _____ = _____

2

$4 \times 3 = $ _____

_____ $\times$ _____ = _____

3

$4 \times 5 = $ _____

_____ $\times$ _____ = _____

4

$3 \times 6 = $ _____

_____ $\times$ _____ = _____

5

$7 \times 3 = $ _____

_____ $\times$ _____ = _____

6

$8 \times 2 = $ _____

_____ $\times$ _____ = _____

7

$2 \times 6 = $ _____

_____ $\times$ _____ = _____

8

$10 \times 2 = $ _____

_____ $\times$ _____ = _____

9

$4 \times 8 = $ _____

_____ $\times$ _____ = _____

10

$5 \times 9 = $ _____

_____ $\times$ _____ = _____

Multiply Across and Down

(1) 2 x 6 = _____   (2) 5 x 4 = _____   (3) 6 x 4 = _____

$$
\begin{array}{r}
2 \\
\times\quad 6 \\
\hline

\end{array}
$$

$$
\begin{array}{r}
\times \\
\hline

\end{array}
$$

$$
\begin{array}{r}
\times \\
\hline

\end{array}
$$

(4) 1 x 8 = _____   (5) 7 x 3 = _____   (6) 5 x 5 = _____

$$
\begin{array}{r}
\times \\
\hline

\end{array}
$$

$$
\begin{array}{r}
\times \\
\hline

\end{array}
$$

$$
\begin{array}{r}
\times \\
\hline

\end{array}
$$

(7) 2 x 9 = _____   (8) 5 x 6 = _____   (9) 8 x 3 = _____

$$
\begin{array}{r}
\times \\
\hline

\end{array}
$$

$$
\begin{array}{r}
\times \\
\hline

\end{array}
$$

$$
\begin{array}{r}
\times \\
\hline

\end{array}
$$

(10) 10 x 5 = _____   (11) 10 x 4 = _____   (12) 8 x 5 = _____

$$
\begin{array}{r}
\times \\
\hline

\end{array}
$$

$$
\begin{array}{r}
\times \\
\hline

\end{array}
$$

$$
\begin{array}{r}
\times \\
\hline

\end{array}
$$

Multiplication Chart

① How many wheels are there on 6 bikes?

Number of bikes	1	2	3	4	5	6
Number of wheels	2	4				

total wheels = _____

② How many corners are there in 5 triangles?

Number of corners	1	2	3	4	5
Number of triangles					

total corners = _____

③ How many fingers are there on 7 hands?

Number of fingers	1	2	3	4	5	6	7
Number of hands							

total fingers = _____

④ How many dots are there on 6 dice?

Number of dice	1	2	3	4	5	6
Number of dots	2	4				

total dots = _____

Equal Shares

1. 12 oranges are put equally into different number of packets. How can the oranges be divided?

Give 2 possible answers. The first one has been done for you.

Number of packets   Oranges in each packet

2	→	6
3	→	
4	→	

2. 10 flowers are put equally into different number of vases. How can the flowers be divided? Give 2 possible answers.

Number of vases   Flowers in each vase

| 2 | → | 6 |
| 5 | → | |

3. 16 balls are put equally into different number of boxes. How can the balls be divided? Give 3 possible answers.

Number of boxes   Balls in each box

Make Equal Groups

Circle the objects to make equal groups. How many groups are there?

① Divide 12 tricycles into groups of 4.

_____ groups

② Divide 15 leaves into groups of 3.

_____ groups

③ Divide 18 books into groups of 6.

_____ groups

④ Divide 24 books into groups of 3.

_____ groups

Subtraction and Division

(1) You have 15 ■ . Make groups of 3.

15	12	9	6	3
- 3	- 3	- 3	- 3	- 3

$15 \div 3 = \underline{\quad}$

(1) You have 20 ■ . Make groups of 5.

20	15	10	5
- 5	- 5	- 5	- 5

$20 \div 5 = \underline{\quad}$

(1) You have 14 ■ . Make groups of 2.

14	12	10	8	6	4	2
- 2	- 2	- 2	- 2	- 2	- 2	- 2

$14 \div 2 = \underline{\quad}$

(1) You have 30 ■ . Make groups of 10.

30	20	10
- 10	- 10	- 10

$30 \div 10 = \underline{\quad}$

NUMBER FRACTIONS

In this chapter, students will learn to:

- Identify simple fractions of a shape, quantity, and set of objects.

- Write simple fractions and sort out smaller or larger fractions.

Explore Fractions

Write the fraction that shows the shaded part.

1 2 equal parts

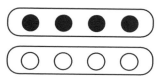

$$\frac{1}{2}$$

2 3 equal parts

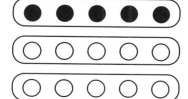

_____

3 4 equal parts

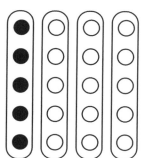

_____

4 3 equal parts

_____

5 2 equal parts

_____

6 4 equal parts

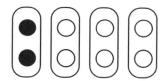

_____

7 5 equal parts

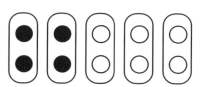

_____

8 6 equal parts

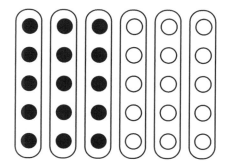

_____

Unit Fractions

Color the leaves to show the fractions.

$\dfrac{1}{4}$

$\dfrac{1}{3}$

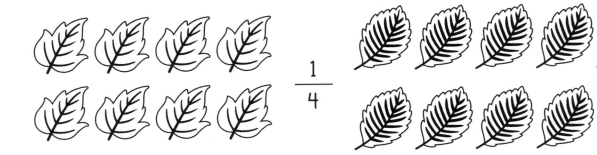

$\dfrac{1}{4}$

$\dfrac{1}{2}$

$\dfrac{1}{8}$

$\dfrac{1}{10}$

More Fractions

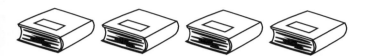

$\dfrac{3}{4}$ yellow and $\dfrac{1}{4}$ blue

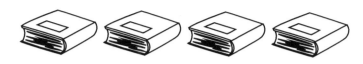

$\dfrac{1}{4}$ green and $\dfrac{3}{4}$ pink

$\dfrac{2}{3}$ purple and $\dfrac{1}{3}$ brown

$\dfrac{1}{3}$ red and $\dfrac{2}{3}$ blue

$\dfrac{2}{5}$ yellow and $\dfrac{3}{5}$ blue

$\dfrac{4}{5}$ yellow and $\dfrac{1}{5}$ blue

$\dfrac{2}{7}$ pink and $\dfrac{5}{7}$ orange

$\dfrac{4}{7}$ green and $\dfrac{3}{7}$ purple

Compare Fractions

1  $\dfrac{3}{3}$

 $\dfrac{1}{3}$

$$\dfrac{3}{3} \; > \; \dfrac{1}{3}$$

true	false

2 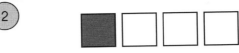 $\dfrac{1}{4}$

$\dfrac{3}{4}$

$$\dfrac{1}{4} \; < \; \dfrac{3}{4}$$

true	false

3  $\dfrac{4}{5}$

$\dfrac{3}{5}$

$$\dfrac{4}{5} \; < \; \dfrac{3}{5}$$

true	false

4  $\dfrac{2}{4}$

$\dfrac{3}{4}$

$$\dfrac{3}{3} \; < \; \dfrac{1}{3}$$

true	false

5 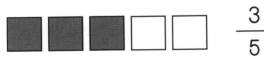 $\dfrac{3}{5}$

 $\dfrac{1}{5}$

$$\dfrac{3}{3} \; > \; \dfrac{1}{3}$$

true	false

6  $\dfrac{4}{6}$

 $\dfrac{5}{6}$

$$\dfrac{3}{3} \; < \; \dfrac{1}{3}$$

true	false

MEASUREMENT

In this chapter, students will learn to:

- Choose and use different non-standard and standard units to measure, calculate, differentiate, and solve word problems related to length (cm, m), weight (g, kg), volume (ml, l).

- Identify and show temperatures in ^{0}C and ^{0}F. Read the thermometer.

- Distinguish whole hour, half hour, quarter hour, 5 minute intervals, tell time differences, solve word problems, daily activities, and estimate time.

Use appropriate measuring tools and make reasonable estimates.

-Read a calendar.

Nonstandard Units

About how many paper clips long is the pencil? Estimate. Then measure with a paper clip to check.

1.

Estimate: About _____ paper clips

Actual: About _____ paper clips

2.

Estimate: About _____ paper clips

Actual: About _____ paper clips

3.

Estimate: About _____ paper clips

Actual: About _____ paper clips

4.

Estimate: About _____ paper clips

Actual: About _____ paper clips

5.

Estimate: About _____ paper clips

Actual: About _____ paper clips

Centimeters and Meters

Which unit would you use to measure the real object?
Circle the better unit of measurement.

1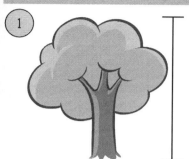

Centimeters

Meters

2

Centimeters

Meters

3

Centimeters

Meters

4

Centimeters

Meters

5

Centimeters

Meters

6

Centimeters

Meters

7

Centimeters

Meters

8

Centimeters

Meters

9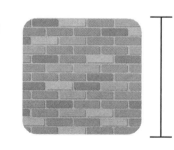

Centimeters

Meters

Centimeters and Meters

Solve the following operations

1. A piece of wire was 35 centimeters long. Another piece measuring 47 centimeters is attached to it. What is the total length of the wire now?

___ cm

Tens	Ones	
		cm
+		cm
		cm

2. Meena has a 73 meter long piece of cloth. Peter has a 65 meter long piece of cloth. How much cloth do they have altogether?

___ m

Tens	Ones	
		m
+		m
		m

3. A ribbon is 96 centimeters long. 52 centimeters of ribbon was cut off. How much ribbon is there left?

___ cm

Tens	Ones	
		cm
−		cm
		cm

4. Carl built a Lego tower that was 88 centimeters tall. It collapsed and now it is only 36 centimeters. How many centimeters shorter is the tower now?

___ cm

Tens	Ones	
		cm
−		cm
		cm

5. Catherine has a 5 centimeter long pencil. How long would 5 pencils be?

___ cm

Tens	Ones	
		cm
X		cm
		cm

Grams and Kilograms

Which unit would you use to measure the weight?
Circle the unit of measurement.

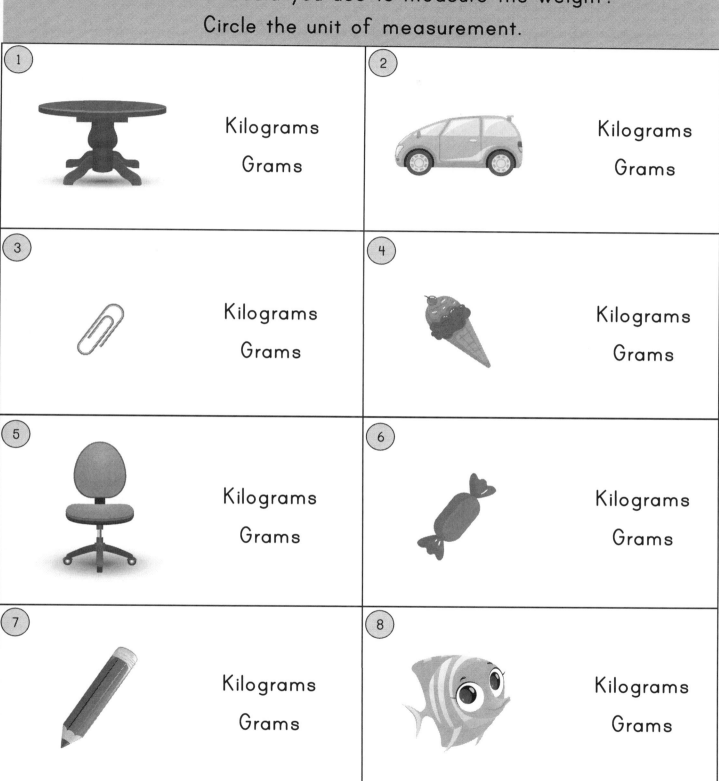

1
Kilograms
Grams

2
Kilograms
Grams

3
Kilograms
Grams

4
Kilograms
Grams

5
Kilograms
Grams

6
Kilograms
Grams

7
Kilograms
Grams

8
Kilograms
Grams

Kilogram and Grams

Solve the following operations.

1. Sandy's recipe calls for 200 grams of flour and 80 grams of sugar. How may grams would it be in total?

   ___ g

Tens	Ones	
		g
+		g
		g

2. A shopkeeper bought 50 kilograms of potatoes and 49 kilograms of tomatoes. How many kilograms of vegetables did he buy altogether?

   ___ Kg

Tens	Ones	
		kg
+		kg
		kg

3. There are 78 kilograms of apples and 36 kilograms of apricot. How much more do the apple weigh?

   ___ Kg

Tens	Ones	
		kg
−		kg
		kg

4. A bag of flour weighs 10 kilograms. What would 2 bags of flour weigh?

   ___ Kg

Tens	Ones	
		kg
X		kg
		kg

5. A packet of candies weigh 50g. What would 3 packets weigh?

   ___ g

Tens	Ones	
		g
X		g
		g

Liters and Milliliters

About how much does the container hold?
Circle the more reasonable estimate.

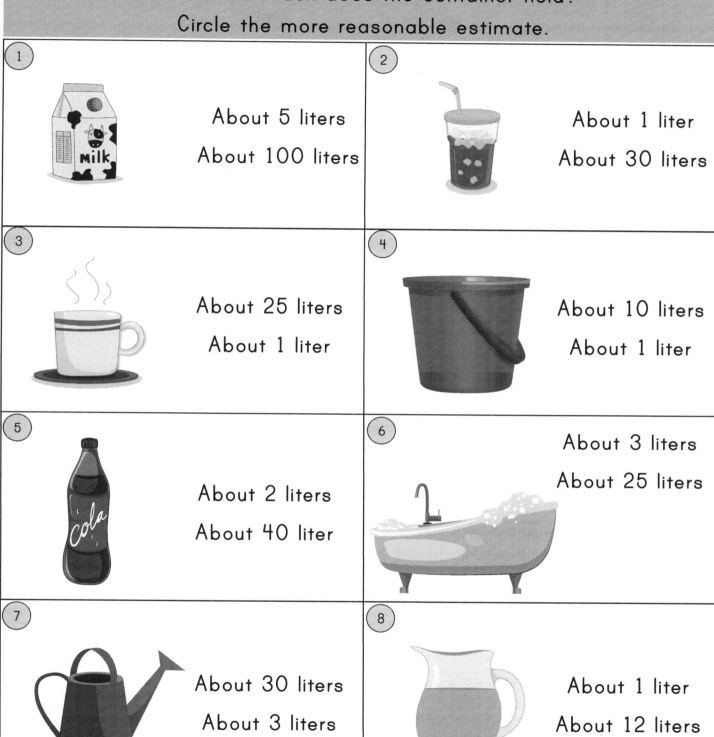

1. About 5 liters

   About 100 liters

2. About 1 liter

   About 30 liters

3. About 25 liters

   About 1 liter

4. About 10 liters

   About 1 liter

5. About 2 liters

   About 40 liter

6. About 3 liters

   About 25 liters

7. About 30 liters

   About 3 liters

8. About 1 liter

   About 12 liters

Liters and Milliliters

Solve the following operations.

1) A fish tank contains 50 liters of water. 25 liters of water are added. What is the total amount of water in the fish tank?

___ l

Tens	Ones
	l
+	l
	l

2) Megan made 95 milliliters of orange juice. Marina made 89 milliliters of orange juice. How much juice did they make altogether?

___ ml

Tens	Ones
	ml
+	ml
	ml

3) A water tank contains 87 liters of water. 43 liters of water are poured out of it. How much water is left in the tank?

___ l

Tens	Ones
	l
-	l
	l

4) A tree needs 2 liters of water in one day. How much water does the tree need in 7 days?

___ l

Tens	Ones
	l
X	l
	l

5) One can of Pepsi can hold 50 millilitres. How much pepsi would 2 cans hold?

___ ml

Tens	Ones
	ml
X	ml
	ml

Temperature

Read the temperature. Use a red crayon to color the thermometer to show the temperature.

1 20 °C

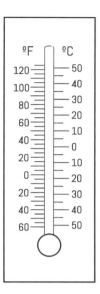

2 80 °F

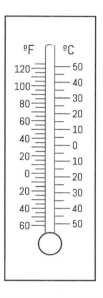

3 10 °C

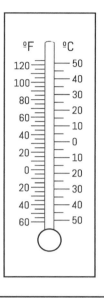

Read the thermometer. Write the temperature.

1

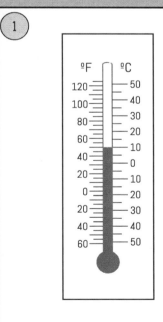

_____ °F

2

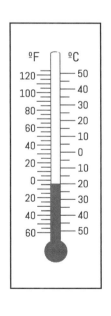

_____ °C

3

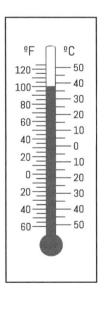

_____ °F

Appropriate Measuring Tool

Choose and write the appropriate measuring tool.

Cup   Thermometer   Ruler   Weight

Make Reasonable Estimates

Circle the most reasonable estimate.

1 Jane has a few parrots. About how many parrots might she have?

3   50   100

2 Eric took out some books from the library. About how many books might that be?

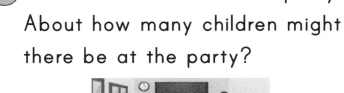

5   50   100

3 Catherine has a large collection of stickers. About how many stickers might she have?

2   20   200

4 Alice went to a class party. About how many children might there be at the party?

5   20   90

5 Brown bought a pack of crayons. About how many crayons might be in the pack?

Crayon

2   12   300

6 Clara put some apples in the bowl. About how many apples might she have put?

10   100   200

Telling Time

_____

_____

_____

_____

_____

_____

_____

_____

_____

_____

_____

_____

80

Telling Time to 5 Minutes

Write the time.

Note: There are 60 minutes in an hour.

(1) 5 minutes after 2:00

_____

(2) 5 minutes after 10:15

_____

(3) 5 minutes after 5:55

_____

(4) 5 minutes after 9:30

_____

(5) 5 minutes before 3:00

_____

(6) 5 minutes before 7:15

_____

(7) 5 minutes before 9:30

_____

(8) 5 minutes before 5:00

_____

Daily Activities

Write the time of each activity that you do by filling in the boxes.
Tick A.M or P.M.

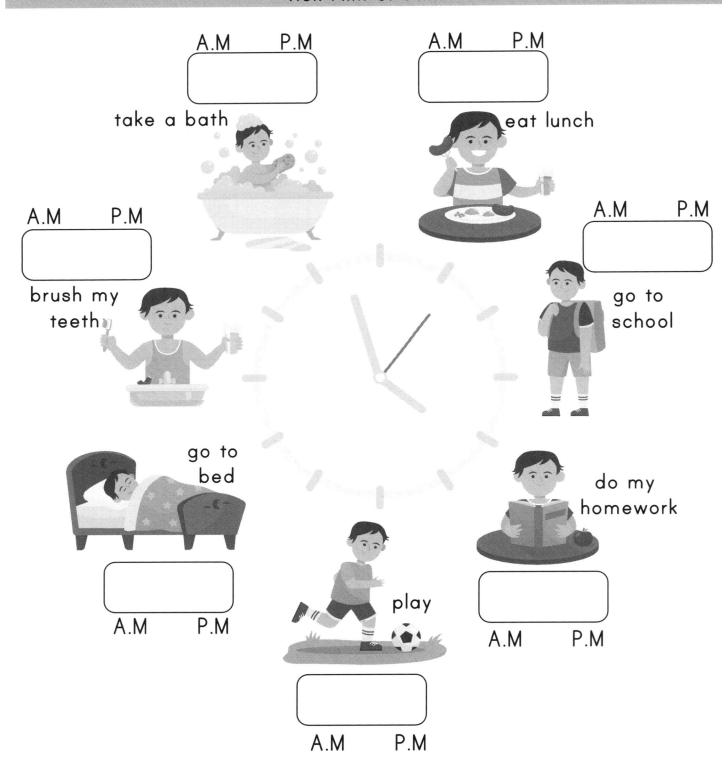

A.M   P.M

take a bath

A.M   P.M

eat lunch

A.M   P.M

brush my
teeth

A.M   P.M

go to
school

go to
bed

A.M   P.M

play

do my
homework

A.M   P.M

A.M   P.M

Estimate Time

About how long will it take? Circle the reasonable estimate.

1 take out the garbage	2 wear the uniform	3 go to school
5 minutes 5 hours	15 minutes 1 hour	5 minutes 5 hours
4 Dust	5 water plants	6 do homework
10 minutes 10 hours	5 hours 5 minutes	20 minutes 1 hour
7 wear shoes	8 eat ice-cream	9 take a snap
2 minutes 2 hours	5 minutes 1 hour	1 minute 1 hour

Time-Word Problems

Use a watch to help solve the problem. Write how much time has passed.

1) Bella begins to play football at 4:30 P.M. She finishes playing at 5:30 P.M. How much time passed?

_____ hour

2) Jeremy delivers newspapers. He begins at 6:00 A.M. He finishes at 7:00 A.M. How much time passed?

_____ hour

3) Anderson begins to read at 4:00 P.M. She finishes the book at 6:00 P.M. How much time passed?

_____ hour

4) Brandon plays with his friends in the yard. He begins at 1:30 P.M. He finishes at 3:30 P.M. How much time passed?

_____ hour

5) Jeena begins to eat lunch at 12:10 P.M. She finishes at 1:10 P.M. How much time passed?

_____ hour

6) Andy takes a nap at 12:00 A.M. He wakes up at 6:00 A.M. How much time passed?

_____ hour

Reading the Calendar

Today's date is _____/_____/_____   The season is _____

What day is it on the...

2nd of February _____   9th of October _____

15th of July _____   20th of November _____

12th of August _____   5th of January _____

9th of September _____   16th of March _____

25th of December _____   30th of June _____

What day is it ...

3 days before the 14th of January _____

1 week from the 3rd of February _____

6 days after the 7th July _____

Which months have 31 days. Write 3 of them.

_____ , _____ , _____

Which months have 30 days. Write 3 of them.

_____ , _____ , _____

Which month has 28 or 29 days _____ .

GEOMETRY

In this chapter, students will learn to:

-Identify, name, recognize different 2D-shapes.

-Compare different shapes on the basis of their sides and corners.

-Describe position and direction.

-Make pictograms and use tally charts to make pictograms.

Shape - Sides and Corners

Shape	Sides	Corners
△		
⬭		
☐		
○		
⬡		
☆		
⬠		
▭		

Color by Shape

Color the following shapes using the given hint.

Rectangle = Blue

 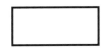 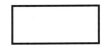 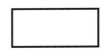

Square = Yellow

Stars = Green

Triangle = Orange

Diamond = Purple

Circle = Pink

Shape Names

_____

_____

_____

_____

Color by Sides

Color these shapes by using the color code and count each of them.

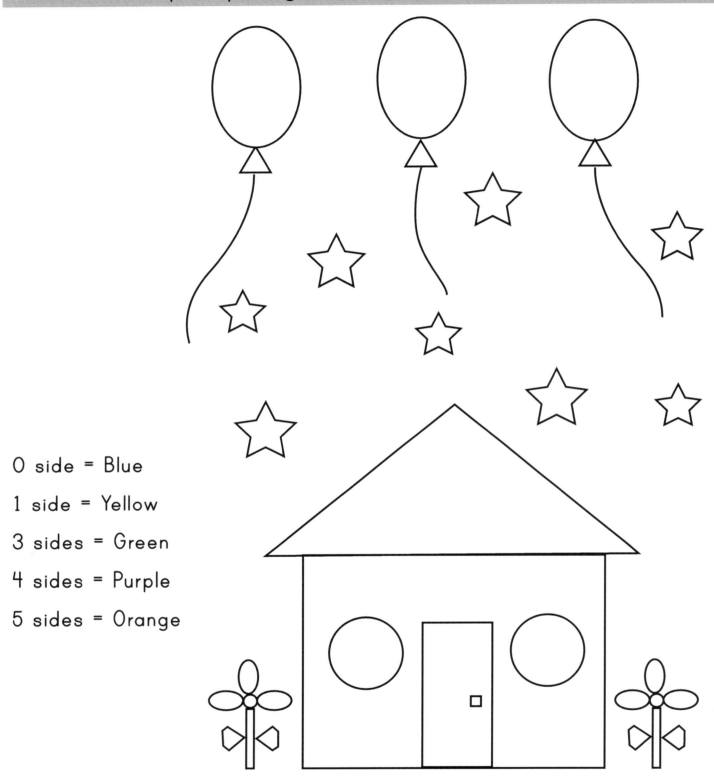

0 side = Blue

1 side = Yellow

3 sides = Green

4 sides = Purple

5 sides = Orange

Directions

East

Noon

Moonrise
Sunset

Moonset
Sunrise

Midnight

91

Pictogram

Count the candies and fill in the graph by coloring one box for each kind of candy.

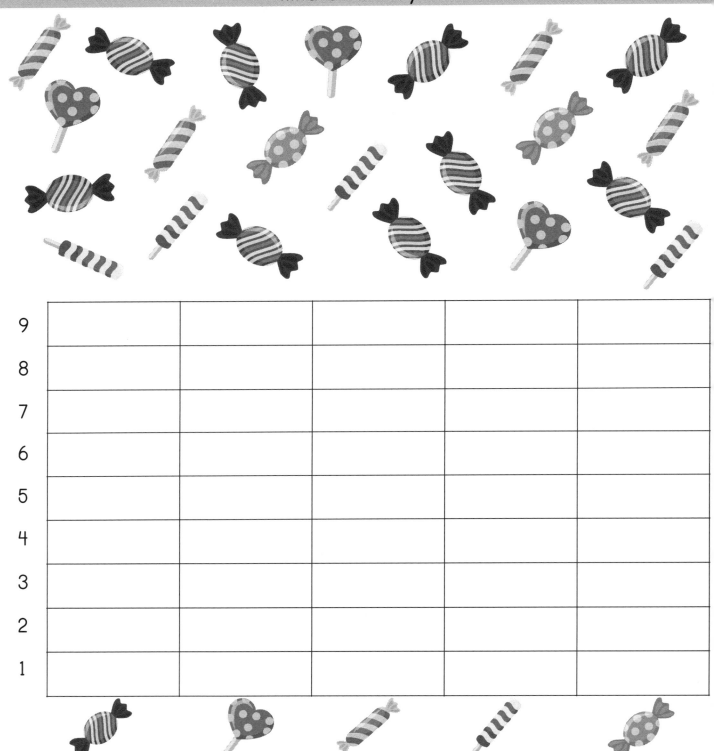

Pictogram

	Favorite Fruit
Pears	🍐 🍐 🍐 🍐
Bananas	🍌 🍌 🍌 🍌 🍌 🍌 🍌 🍌
Peaches	🍑 🍑
Strawberries	🍓 🍓 🍓 🍓 🍓 🍓 🍓 🍓 🍓 🍓 🍓
Apples	🍎 🍎 🍎 🍎 🍎 🍎 🍎

Which is the favorite for most people?

_____

Which is the favorite for fewer people?

_____

How many more people like apples than pears?

_____

How many more people like bananas than apples?

_____

How many fewer people like peaches than pears?

_____

Tally Chart

Tally Chart:

Pictorgram:

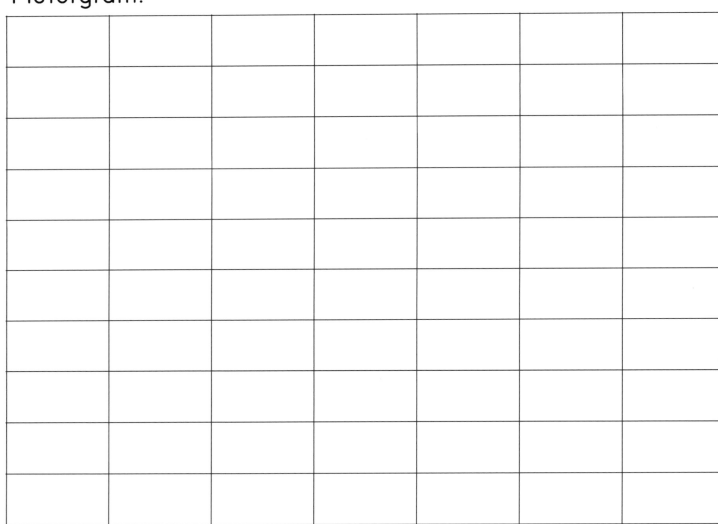

Other books from Brainchild you could find on Amazon

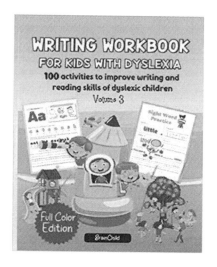

Made in United States
Orlando, FL
15 April 2022

16864435R00057